The Best Seats in the House

Story by Fiona Hardy

Illustrations by Katie Kear

The Best Seats in the House

Text: Fiona Hardy
Publishers: Tania Mazzeo and Eliza Webb
Series consultant: Amanda Sutera
Hands on Heads Consulting
Editor: Jess Mackay
Project editor: Annabel Smith
Designer: Jess Kelly
Project designer: Danielle Maccarone
Illustrations: Katie Kear
Production controller: Renee Tome

NovaStar

ISBN 978 0 17 033473 0

Cengage Learning Australia
Level 5, 80 Dorcas Street
Southbank VIC 3006 Australia
Phone: 1300 790 853
Email: aust.nelsonprimary@cengage.com

For learning solutions, visit **cengage.com.au**

Printed in China by 1010 Printing International Ltd
1 2 3 4 5 6 7 29 28 27 26 25

Nelson acknowledges the Traditional Owners and Custodians of the lands of all First Nations Peoples. We pay respect to Elders past and present, and extend that respect to all First Nations Peoples today.

Contents

HOLBERRY COMMUNIT
FOOTBALL DAY!
EVERYONE WELCOME!

Chapter 1

Finishing Touches

By the time Jade and Mitch finished painting the last letter on their sign, it was getting dark. They could see stars twinkling against the red sky above the football oval.

"You know what they say about a red sky at night," Coach Craighill said, coming up beside where the two kids were sitting on the grass. "It means the weather will be great tomorrow for the community footy day, after our recent rain. You two have worked so hard on this."

Jade and Mitch looked down proudly at all they'd done. The sign was going to hang across the entrance to their town's football oval. It said: HOLBERRY COMMUNITY FOOTBALL DAY! EVERYONE WELCOME!

Jade and Mitch loved Australian Rules football. They had known each other since they'd both joined the Holberry Bolts preschool team. Mitch had watched Jade's face light up when she kicked her first ever goal, and he knew they'd be best friends.

They watched as many local football games as they could, especially Holberry's senior team matches. Last year, Jade and Mitch had even made the three-hour trip to the city with their families to watch an Australian Football League Women's semi-final. They'd been able to see their favourite player, Emma Atherfold, who grew up not far from Holberry, though their seats were so high up that Emma had looked like a tiny speck on the big ground.

Community Football Day was a fundraiser to help improve the Holberry Bolts' clubrooms. The old ones were worn-out portable classrooms from the primary school, and they still had times-tables posters glued to the walls. Mitch said it should be illegal to have to look at maths on weekends.

The new clubrooms would have ramps instead of stairs, a gym and a big room for football-club celebrations. There would even be new stands around the ground, which meant a lot more seating for everyone.

The Holberry Bolts women's football team had won the regional grand final this year, and the whole town had celebrated. Tomorrow, to help support the community day, the same team was going to play an exhibition match against the Mullum Brumbies, who won their grand final in the Mullum region. People were planning to come from all over the state. It was going to be a great game, and Jade and Mitch couldn't wait.

Coach Craighill smiled down at Jade and Mitch. “Come with me,” he said. “I have something to show you.”

He led them across the brown grass and past all the market stalls set up for tomorrow. Jade's family, who owned a peach orchard, was going to be there during the day, selling peach-flavoured cupcakes and peach iced tea. They strolled past the stage where Mitch's mum was going to play in her band. Next, they walked past all the footy-themed games, like the kicking competition Jade and Mitch had painted the target for.

Finally, Coach Craighill took them up to the old stands. He led them to the row of seats at the back, the best view of all, and pointed.

Two seats had signs on them. One said JADE ALI. The other said MITCHELL PHELAN.

"After all your hard work over the past few weeks," Coach Craighill said, "you deserve the best seats in the house to watch the game."

Jade and Mitch squealed and gave each other a fist bump, then gave Coach Craighill a respectful grown-up handshake and said thank you. They sat in their seats and looked out over the ground.

“Plus,” Coach Craighill said, “I thought it would be good for you to have a nice view of our special guest playing tomorrow.”

“A special guest?” Jade asked warily. “Like that time our principal tried to join in without knowing the rules and brought a cricket bat?”

“No principals,” Coach Craighill said, laughing. “I mean Emma Atherfold.”

Jade and Mitch started yelling. “What? Emma Atherfold? *The* Emma Atherfold?”

“The one and only,” Coach Craighill said. “She wanted to help support women’s football in small towns like the one she grew up in. We only just found out she could make it.”

Jade and Mitch couldn’t believe it. They were going to be sitting here, in the best seats, watching their favourite player.

Tomorrow was going to be the best day ever.

Chapter 2

Horsing Around

Mitch and his parents drove to Community Football Day early the next morning. Coach Craighill had been right about the weather: it was warm, and the sky was clear. As they drove along the dusty streets, their little town slowly woke up around them.

When they arrived, people were already walking under the big sign Jade and Mitch had made. There was a new sign stuck to the end that said: GUEST PLAYER: EMMA ATHERFOLD!

Mitch felt his skin prickle with excitement.

They walked to the stage where the band was going to play. Mitch's parents were helping out there all day and said they'd be right by the stage whenever Mitch needed them. Mitch waved goodbye and ran to the market stalls to find his best friend.

HOLBERRY COMMUNITY FOOTBALL DAY!
EVERYONE WELCOME!
GUEST PLAYER: EMMA ATHERFOLD!

Jade's family had already set up their stall. Jade was behind the counter, taking money from all the people buying cupcakes and iced tea.

"Mitch!" she said when she saw him. "I can't believe we're going to see Emma Atherfold today!"

"Me neither!" Mitch said.

Jade's dad said, "I know you two have been saving up your pocket money for today. You go have fun until the game starts at midday." He gave them both a cupcake and said, "You've earned it!"

Jade and Mitch smiled at each other and ran into the crowd.

They had the best morning. They each got a Holberry Bolts t-shirt with the logo on the front. They bought some hand-drawn local football cards. They cheered for Mitch's mum playing guitar in her band. They played all the sports-themed games until they were almost out of gold coins. Jade was so good at kicking that she could put a football right through a target.

They watched the crowds fill up around the ground for the game but knew they didn't have to worry. Their perfect spot would be waiting for them.

At twelve o'clock, they went up to their seats, high up at the back with the best view of the entire footy ground. All the other seats were full. They were sitting just behind a row of teenagers in the opposition's colours.

Jade and Mitch smiled at the signs with their names and settled in to wait for the game to begin.

Players were starting to run out onto the ground. Soon, they'd see Emma Atherfold. They were on the edge of their seats, excited to see their favourite player up close.

Then the teenagers in front of Mitch and Jade reached down into the bags at their feet and pulled out horse-head hats that looked just like the wild brown brumbies that sometimes roamed outside of their town. Each teenager put on a horse head, and they cheered, "Gooooo, Brumbies!"

The heads were big, with tall pointy ears. Jade and Mitch couldn't see over them.

Then somebody beside them gasped. "It's Emma Atherfold!"

The whole crowd went wild.

But Jade and Mitch couldn't see anything.

"Em-ma! Em-ma!" everyone chanted.

"Maybe we should say something about the hats?" Jade said.

Mitch leant forward, just as the teenagers in front called out, "Go Brumbies! We're coming for all the Bolts!"

They started stomping and hooting loudly.

Mitch sat back, looking a little afraid. “Maybe not,” he said to Jade.

They looked at each other miserably.

“We’re going to have to move,” Jade said.

They got up out of their seats, looking back at their names sadly. The seats had been so perfect, but there was no other choice.

The siren sounded. The game was about to start.

Chapter 3

The Game Begins

Down at ground level, everybody was buzzing. The stand had fewer than fifty seats, so most spectators were standing around the boundary fence. There was usually more than enough space, but today it felt like everybody from Holberry all the way to the Mullum region and everywhere in between was here. It made the air electric with excitement, but it made Mitch and Jade even sadder that they couldn't see their hero play.

"We've got to find a space somewhere," Jade said anxiously.

They heard a whistle – the game was starting. Above the people crowded against the boundary fence, they saw the first bounce of the ball into the air. There was the thump of the ball on a player's boot, and the crowd roared with excitement.

"There!" Mitch yelled.

He pointed to an empty spot between two people. It was barely big enough for one person, but they both managed to squeeze in.

They could see now, almost. There was an umpire standing right in front of them, in a bright yellow jacket. Either side of the umpire, they could just see some players running around.

This game wasn't turning out at all like they had hoped.

"Thbs s fn," Mitch said.

"Wt?" Jade asked.

They were so squashed they couldn't even speak properly. Jade thought she saw Emma's leg appear next to the umpire. In excitement, she squealed, "Mma!" so loud that she popped right out of her spot.

"Are you okay?" Mitch asked, catching her.

Jade nodded, and tried to squeeze back in. Mitch growled at her.

"I'm sorry!" she said. "I'm trying! Don't growl at me!"

"I didn't!" Mitch said, but then he made the same sound again. They both looked down at his stomach and then at each other.

"Oh," Mitch said. "I guess I did growl at you."

That was when Jade realised she was hungry, too. They hadn't eaten anything since the cupcakes earlier that morning.

The people they were squashing up against had a picnic basket filled with pies and hot jam doughnuts. They smelled amazing. Jade started leaning so close to the food that Mitch had to catch her before she fell in face-first.

"Let's go to the canteen," Mitch said. "I think we can see better from up there anyway, and we can get some food at the same time."

Mitch was right. The queue for the canteen was long, but it was up on a narrow hill, and for the first time that day they could clearly see Emma Atherfold, running as fast as lightning across the field. They grabbed each other in excitement as Emma leapt into the sky near the goals and caught the ball.

The crowd erupted. “What an awesome mark!” Mitch yelled.

Now that Emma had the ball, she took a moment to set up for a goal. If she got it square through the middle two posts, she’d add six points to the Bolts’ score, putting the team in the lead. She adjusted her socks, took a deep breath, spun the ball in her hands, then started the run-up and –

“Excuse me,” the woman in line behind them said, “can you please keep moving?”

Mitch and Jade had stopped for so long that they’d held up the queue. They apologised and stepped forward, behind a tree and out of sight of the ground. Around them, the crowd went wild, yelling, “GOOOOAL!”

Emma had kicked the goal, but Jade and Mitch hadn’t even seen her do it. They stared at each other, devastated.

“I can’t believe we missed it,” Mitch said.

“It’s okay,” Jade said, though she didn’t believe her own words.

Jade and Mitch finally made it to the counter. They ordered a bag of donuts and some hot chips with the last of their spending money. Once they had their food, they trudged back down to the oval to hunt for a good spot.

Further around the fence, away from the goals, Jade spotted a group of people sitting on the ground with space around them.

Then Mitch said, "Um, what does that person have on their shoulder?"

Jade squinted. "Is that a ... bird?"

Chapter 4

Flying High

It was a bird. It was a big blue-and-grey parrot, perched on a woman's shoulder. When it saw Mitch and Jade, it squawked.

"He's friendly," the woman under the parrot said. "His name is Noodle."

Jade went up to Noodle and gently touched his feathery back. He squawked again and said, "Go the Parrots!"

"He thinks all football teams are called the Parrots," the woman said. "He was really excited to come to this game and watch the Bolts win."

"Emma!" Noodle cawed. "Emma Parrot!"

"Emma Atherfold is his favourite," the woman added.

Just then, Mitch and Jade realised that there were a lot of pets in this area of the ground.

There were dogs of all shapes and sizes, and somebody even had a cat on a leash, though it was asleep on its owner's feet.

"This spot is perfect," Mitch said happily, finding some space between two dogs and sitting down with Jade.

For a moment, they were lost in the game. All the players were fast and strong. Emma Atherfold was even faster, and it seemed like she was everywhere on the ground at the same time. If the Bolts had the ball, she was nearby to mark it. If the Brumbies had the ball, she was running after them, and tackling them to the ground.

“This is like a dream,” Jade said, sighing with pleasure. “I can’t believe she’s really here in front of us.” Then, like Mitch, her stomach growled. The fluffy white dog next to her looked up in alarm.

Mitch laughed. “We’ve got the perfect view now. Warm donuts, good footy – it’s the best day ever.” He got a doughnuts out of the bag and went to take a bite.

Suddenly, there was a flurry of fur and chaos and Mitch no longer had a doughnuts in his hand.

"Sorry!" said a man nearby. "My dog really likes donuts."

The sausage dog that stole the food didn't look even slightly guilty. Mitch laughed and said, "It's okay."

He moved his bag to his other side and got out another doughnuts. Straight away, there was a burst of fur and slobber, and then Mitch lost another one.

"Sorry!" a kid behind him called out. "My dog likes donuts, too."

Just then, Jade opened her box of chips. They were salty and hot. Her stomach flipped with hunger. She took out a chip. Then, careful to avoid all dogs, she held the box out to Mitch.

This time, the chaos came from above. There were a lot of feathers and wings flapping, and half of the chips ended up spread all over the ground.

"Sorry!" said the woman with the parrot, looking horrified. "Maybe Noodle is *too* friendly."

One of the dogs was licking the spilled salt off Jade's bare legs. She and Mitch looked at each other in sorrow and sighed.

"Time to move again?" Mitch asked.

"Time to move," Jade agreed.

Chapter 5

Aim for the Sky

Jade and Mitch ate the rest of their doughnuts and chips as they walked slowly around the oval, feeling more heartbroken with each step. All they could hear was cheering from the crowd, the **thunk** of the ball being kicked and people talking about how incredible the game was. They were upset that they couldn't watch the game they'd worked so hard to help plan.

Having Emma Atherfold this close, but too far away to see, felt unfair. Jade and Mitch still remembered being at Jade's house, watching Emma's first game on TV, and seeing Jade's mum cry with joy.

"When I was little," Jade's mum had said, "I wanted to play footy so much, but I wasn't allowed to, because I was a girl. A girl just like Emma, who loved to play.

“When I see her play, it makes me happy to think girls don’t have to hear that they can’t play any more.”

Jade liked that memory, even though it hurt her heart a little bit. Mitch thought about it every time the commentator said Emma’s name. Seeing her close up would have been amazing, but now it felt like they wouldn’t see her at all.

Jade thought she was just about to cry when Mitch grabbed her arm and pulled her to a spot at the boundary fence, right near the Brumbies' goal.

The spot was wide enough for the two of them, but there was one big problem. A giant sign advertising Papa Marco's Pizza was right in front of them. It was tall enough for grown-ups to see over, but not Jade and Mitch.

"I have an idea," Mitch said. "We can take it in turns." He crouched down and said, "Get on my shoulders!"

"Are you sure?" Jade asked warily. "It's still muddy here from the rain on Friday."

"Come on," Mitch said. "It'll be fine."

Jade hopped on his back. He straightened up, and she gasped.

Jade could see Emma nearby – in real life, almost within reach.

The Brumbies had control of the ball, and were kicking it to each other, while dodging the Bolts players, who were leaping for it. Emma ran off, towards the ball, and Jade was breathless with happiness watching her intercept it so smoothly. Emma kicked the ball to another Bolts player, who fumbled it. A Brumbies player picked it up and ran back again.

"Let's swap!" Jade called down to Mitch. "Maybe you can watch the Bolts get a goal."

They took turns for a few minutes, climbing on each other's shoulders and getting muddy footprints on each other's new t-shirts. It was worth it to be up there, seeing the game they loved.

"What's happening now?" Mitch called up to Jade when the crowd started cheering.

"Everyone's fighting for the ball!" Jade said.

"My turn! Hang onto the fence to get down," Mitch said, letting go of Jade's legs just as she yelled, "Emma's got it!" and threw her hands in the air.

They tumbled down onto the muddy ground. Jade landed right on Mitch and Mitch gave a big **oof!** before she rolled off him.

They both lay on the ground, dirty, sore and sad. Nothing was going their way.

Mitch covered his face with his hands and said, “Maybe I should just go and see if Mum and Dad are ready to go home.”

“Maybe they could drop me off on the way,” Jade said, wishing the ground would swallow her up.

"Are you two all right?" asked a voice they recognised.

"Coach Craighill!" Mitch said.

Jade shook out her arms, and said, "Not really."

Coach helped them up. They were very muddy.

"What's going on?" he asked.

"We can't see the game properly, no matter where we go," Jade said. "We've been all over the ground."

"You've been waiting for this game for weeks. Why aren't you in your seats?" Coach Craighill asked, pointing to the stand.

They all looked up at their seats. To Jade and Mitch's disbelief, the seats were still empty. They looked at each other and grinned.

"I think it's time to go back," Jade said.

Chapter 6

Back from Behind

The siren rang out for the quarter-time break just as Jade and Mitch finished rinsing the mud off their faces from the outside taps. They made their way back through the crowds and up the stairs to their seats in the stand. Jade and Mitch picked up their signs and sat back down behind the brumby heads.

"At least now we're not holding up any queues," Mitch said.

"Or getting licked by dogs," Jade said.

"Or having our food stolen by parrots," Mitch added.

"Or falling off a fence into the mud!" Jade went on, laughing.

The teenagers in their giant brumby-head hats turned around to look at them.

“We were wondering where you two went,” one of them said. “You have personalised seats, and you left them!”

Jade and Mitch exchanged a glance. The teenagers seemed calmer now, and friendly. The answer to their problems seemed embarrassingly obvious.

"Hey," Mitch said. "Do you think you could take your horse heads off when the game starts again?"

"We can't see anything," Jade added. "And we're Emma Atherfold's biggest fans."

"Hmm," another teenager said, looking at his friends. "I don't know."

"Please," Jade said. "We really can't see."

There was a twinkle in the teenager's eye. "I meant that I don't know if you're her biggest fans," he said. "I'm her brother, Adam. I think I'm probably her biggest fan."

"You're her *brother*?" Mitch yelled.

"I am," Adam said. "That's why I'm wearing the brumby head. If she's playing for the Bolts, then I barrack for the other team. That's what brothers do, right?"

The siren blew again. The second quarter was about to start. Adam and his friends took off their brumby heads.

Jade and Mitch now had a view of the whole ground. They could see the huge crowd, building up into a roar of excitement. They could see the players calling encouragement to each other. Emma Atherfold, the greatest player ever, waited right in the middle of the ground with her hands outstretched, to leap for the ball.

"Tell you what," Adam said. "Since you missed out on a quarter of the game because I was trying to annoy my sister, I'll make you a deal. If you tell us the rest of the story about the parrot at half-time, I'll introduce you to Emma after the game."

Jade and Mitch grabbed each other's hands and squeezed.

"For real?" Jade whispered.

"For real," Adam said.

Jade and Mitch looked at each other.

"It's a deal," they said.

Then they settled in to watch the game of the year, in the best seats in the house.